Money Management and Budgeting Hacks

Money Management and Budgeting Hacks

Money Management and Budgeting Hacks

15 Simple Practical Hacks to Manage, Budget and Save Money

Life 'n' Hack

Copyright © Life 'n' Hack

All rights reserved.

It is impermissible to reproduce any part of this book without prior consent. All violations will be prosecuted to the fullest extent of the law.

While attempts have been made to verify the information contained within this publication, neither the author nor the publisher assumes any responsibility for errors, omissions, interpretation or usage of the subject matter herein.

This publication contains the opinions and ideas of its author and is intended for informational purpose only. The author and publisher shall in no event held be liable for any loss or other damages incurred from the usage of this publication.

ISBN 978-1-544-92325-3

Printed in the United States of America

First Edition

KEYS

INFO INTRO: Irresponsible Money Misplacement

- 9 -

HACK #1: Categorize Expenses into Necessities or Discretionary

- 14 -

HACK #2: Create Quickie Budget Chart

- 17 -

HACK #3: Readjust Spending Habits

- 20 -

HACK #4: Prioritize Financial Goals

- 24 -

HACK #5: Baby Steps for NON-Trust Fund Babies

- 27 -

HACK #6: Commit to Tracking Money Relationship

- 33 -

HACK #7: Mint Condition Budgeting

- 35 -

HACK #8: The Cash Envelope Method

- 37 -

HACK #9: The Percentage Pie Method

- 41 -

HACK #10: Open Several Bank Accounts for Specialized Purposes

- 44 -

HACK #11: Use Credit Smartly, not Stupidly

- 47 -

HACK #12: Save Big Bucks by Avoiding Loans

- 51 -

HACK #13: Know "Good Debt" from "Bad Debt"

- 54 -

HACK #14: Invest for the Future Now

- 57 -

HACK #15: Proudly Put on Frugal Hat and Wear It with Pride
- 60 -
(BONUS) HACK #16: Yield 20x Higher Interest with Online Banks
- 62 -
(ADVANCED BONUS) HACK #17: Go from Newbie Investor to Building Wealth the Smart Investor's Way
- 66 -
(ADVANCED BONUS) HACK #18: Diversify Money into Alternative Savings Accounts
- 72 -
INFO UNLOCKED: Wiser Money Management
- 75 -

Money Management and Budgeting Hacks

INFO INTRO:
Irresponsible Money Misplacement

Why budget?

Chances are, if you have to ask this question you're already plagued by money struggles and feeling just a bit scared whenever you open "that next bill." Finances are a leading cause of broken marriages and lie at the root of a lot of depression and anxiety. Many of us, even if we're making decent money, are just one missed paycheck away from disaster.

For some people, the unexpected — a sudden illness, loss of a job, change in the family situation — can lead to a financial crisis. But for millions of us, that crisis is like a slow train wreck, with us sitting in the engineer's chair blithely watching the passing scenery instead of noticing the truck packed with explosives that's stalled across the tracks just ahead. Month after month, we spend a little more than we're earning on things we want — one more Christmas gift, one more nice vacation, those designer shoes on sale this week only — and before you know it, those credit cards are maxing out and we're barely paying the minimum, or maybe missing payments altogether.

Oops. Now what? Uh-oh, here comes that dreaded word: **budgeting.**

Many people think budgeting isn't for them, because it smacks of Mom warning you not to spend all your allowance on candy. It means deprivation, or it's too complicated, or it's just too much effort, or you're expecting to win the lottery next week and it won't matter. That's why so many people continue to make irresponsible decisions about their spending and end up deep in debt, or worse yet, forced out of their homes because they can no longer pay the mortgage or rent.

How is it some people manage to live comfortably and happily on relatively modest earnings, while other people making big bucks are (secretly) in hock up to their eyeballs and terrified? Obviously, the carefree folks have learned a thing or two about managing their money.

Strategies for handling your money well aren't something you automatically pick up by a certain age. In fact, if you weren't fortunate enough to have someone teach you these skills as a kid, it's something you need to take steps to learn.

Here's why:

- Learning how to manage your money helps you save for the future — for unexpected expenses or goals that take a lot of cash, like a car, a house or a nice vacation. When you get into the habit of saving part of what you earn every month, you'll have more options when it comes to that big purchase.

- Learning to create and stick to a budget helps you rely less on credit cards and more on what's already in your pocket or in your bank account. If everyone learned to budget early in life, getting into unmanageable debt would be rare.

- Learning to budget helps you take care of your bills efficiently and effectively. So when the dreaded bills arrive, you won't try to dodge them and end up missing your payments, thus incurring late fees.

- Learning to control cash flow will allow you to know exactly how much you are spending, how much you are saving, and how much you'll need to attain a certain goal (all of which might also help you to make other decisions, for example, whether to get a second job, or when to retire).

When you learn to manage your own money applying these strategies, you'll feel a lot wiser, like a smart banker taking charge of funds that once belonged to an irresponsible person.

Let's move on to our first money management hack.

HACK #1:

Categorize Expenses into Necessities or Discretionary

Amazingly, a lot of people really have no idea where all their money is going. Even though few of us walk around with a load of actual cash these days, we might as well have holes in every pocket in terms of how quickly our earnings seem to disappear.

The first step to seizing control of your money involves a one-month project, starting on the first day of the month:

1. First, pay close attention to your spending over the month, keeping every single receipt to get a good idea of where your money is going. (If you use credit cards,

your credit card bill can be a handy way to collect information too.)

2. Using a cellphone app or a simple paper-and-pencil list, keep track of all your regular EXPENSES for that month: grocery and gasoline receipts, rent, insurance, loan/credit card repayments, donations, monthly bills such as utilities, cable, cellphone, etc. If you take out cash, keep the receipt from the ATM and carefully record how you use the cash.

3. As you're recording these expenses, divide them into two separate lists, one for necessities and one for discretionary spending — things you could survive without if you really had to. Rent and groceries are necessities, for example; movie tickets and lipstick are discretionary spending.

4. At the end of the month add up those amounts to determine your monthly living expenses: necessities and discretionary spending. If you think this was a fairly

average month for you, this can form the basis of your plan for the future. (If not, you may need to keep track for another month or two to get a more realistic idea.) If you have certain expenses, such as property tax, that you only pay periodically, figure out how much these cost over a year and divide by 12 to come to your monthly average.

HACK #2:
Create Quickie Budget Chart

Now listen up — this isn't as difficult as it may sound. You can use an Excel spreadsheet or other software to create a quickie budget chart, though many people find it easiest to grasp when they begin the old-fashioned way, with a sheet of lined paper and a pencil.

1. On the left in a vertical column, list each of the specific expenses you've been tracking, one per line. List them under the big categories: Housing; Utilities; Transportation; Food; Clothing; Personal (insurance, pharmacy, toiletries, entertainment, etc.) Don't forget charitable donations or gifts if those are part of your regular spending.

2. To the right of your listed expenses, create several new columns. In the first, enter or write down what you spent during your testing month, something like this:

HOUSING
Mortgage	$1500

UTILITIES
Electricity	$150
Water	$45
Gas	$132

TRANSPORTATION
Gasoline	$140
Car insurance	$95
Maintenance	$160
Auto loan/lease	$250

FOOD
Groceries	$450
Coffee shop	$135

Restaurants/takeout $530

… and so on. Adapt this to your own spending!

ASSIGNMENT: Now, get out your calculator to add up all your spending, and enter the total at the bottom of the column. Check your pay stubs and add up your earnings for the month. Write or enter that on the line below your total spending amount. Compare the two amounts.

Now it's time for action using these two derived amounts in our next HACK #3.

HACK #3:
Readjust Spending Habits

In the last ASSIGNMENT for HACK #2, if it shows that you've spent most of or even more than you earned for the month, you will need to make some hard choices about where you can either cut spending or increase your earnings.

HOUSING
Mortgage $1500

UTILITIES
Electricity $150
Water $45
Gas $132

TRANSPORTATION
Gasoline $140

Car insurance	$95
Maintenance	$160
Auto loan/lease	$250

<u>FOOD</u>

Groceries	$450
Coffee shop	$135
Restaurants/takeout	$530

1. Take a good look at your list and see where the easiest place is to start curbing your temptation to spend. HINT: It's often from your "discretionary" list. If you spent a lot on coffee, as in this example, consider whether skipping out on your morning latte at Starbuck's, or better yet making your own coffee at home or work, could help you balance your budget. If you're spending a lot on groceries but find yourself tossing out food that's spoiled in your fridge, consider ways to buy less and use what you do buy more efficiently. (Buying bulk at Costco is only worth it if you're actually going to use that giant tub of

mayonnaise!) If you're spending too much on utilities, figure out ways to conserve — and do the Earth a favor, too.

2. In the second column on your budget chart, enter your new target amount for each category. Your rent isn't going to change, but some of your discretionary spending should. Your goal is to make sure that the total at the bottom of this column equals your earnings, MINUS at LEAST 10%. (That means if your earnings for the month are $5000, your total spending should be no more than $4500.)

3. If, no matter what you do, you really can't figure out how to make these numbers work for you, it may be time to look for some secondary income. That's way beyond the scope of this, but at least now you know what you need to do. While you're looking for that second job, you can use this chart to help you cut down as much as possible on discretionary spending, and keep the damage to your financial health at a minimum.

When you're better able to meet your basic needs, it will be easier to figure out how to manage your extra income well.

If you've earned more than you spent, good for you. But chances are there wasn't a lot left over. You should still go through your numbers and see where you might want to set lower goal amounts for certain kinds of spending. Then you have decisions to make about what to do with the money left over. HINT: Save! Save! Save! More on that later.

ASSIGNMENT: Hang on to your quickie budget chart; you will need this later. In future months, you can use the empty columns on the right to continue tracking your actual spending and see whether you are meeting your goals.

HACK #4:
Prioritize Financial Goals

We're all unique, and have our own special hopes and dreams. This is the fun part: instead of just wishing you could win the lottery (not gonna happen, sorry!), start figuring out what you most want (within reason) and then plan your financial future around it.

Your goals might include short-term and long-term items:

- getting out of debt
- saving for a car or other big purchase
- buying a home
- having some money to invest
- paying off student loans
- saving for kids' college or retirement

1. Now put a number to each of these goals. How much will it cost? How much will you need to save each month/year to get there? Is it realistic? You may be surprised at how tucking a little money away every month, in a disciplined way, can add up over the long run.

2. Whatever you decide, go back to your quickie budget chart and add, under the goal column totals, another couple of rows with the heading SAVINGS. Beneath that, write down, one per line, the amount you will designate to each of your current savings goals (e.g. "Pay off Debt"; "Buy a Car"; "Emergency Fund"). From the 10% or more left over after your expenses are tallied, set yourself a goal — an exact dollar amount — for each line. Next month, be sure to deposit that amount into the appropriate account.

Knowing what you want and what it will take to get there will help give you the motivation to rein in your spending, corral that debt that keeps you from achieving your dreams, and save the money it takes to live the life you really want.

Yes, you can get there. But it starts with baby steps.

HACK #5:

Baby Steps for NON-Trust Fund Babies

Unless you were one of the few lucky ones born as trust fund babies, here's how to get your financial life in order, in a series of baby steps as you learn the skills of handling your money. (This may take you a few months or even a few years, but hang in there!)

BABY STEP 1: Build a safety net. If you're struggling, some sense of financial security is essential to your mental health. Start by using the cash you have saved using HACK #3 to create an emergency fund. It doesn't have to be huge, but $1,000 to $2,000 tucked away in an interest-earning savings account, depending on your income, should be your first goal.

BABY STEP 2: Deal with your debts (except for your mortgage — that one is probably with you for a while!). Once you have an emergency fund, start whittling away at those ongoing debts. If you have many kinds of consumer debt — an auto loan, an old student loan, credit card bills carrying over one month to the next — make a list of the outstanding amounts, along with the interest rate you're paying on each (you can find that information, listed as APR, on your bill or statement), and the monthly minimum payment. Remember, interest is your enemy when you're in debt, but it's your friend when you're putting money into savings, so it's a huge advantage when you can turn the situation around.

Now, let's figure out how to bring those suckers down. There are two tactics for paying off debts.

- **The Snowball Method.** If you're feeling a lot of anxiety about debt, this can be a very encouraging way to proceed. You simply start with the debt that's smallest, and pay that off first, while making just the monthly minimum payments on the others. When you get the smallest debt out of the way, move on to the next-smallest. As you see these bills cleared off your plate, you'll feel encouraged. You're making headway! You can do this!

- **The Interest Rate Method.** This will save you the most money in the long run. Pay off the debt with the highest interest rate first, while making minimum payments on the others. When that one's cleared off, pay off the one with the second-highest rate. It gets easier and easier to pay them off, because the amount that interest was adding to your debt is rapidly being reduced.

Once you have debt under control, move on to saving some of your hard-earned cash.

BABY STEP 3: Save enough to cover three to four months' expenses.

- Having serious money put aside for emergencies will be a lifesaver when you have unexpected expenses such as recovering from an accident or serious illness, you lose your job, or you are adjusting to life finding new work and fluctuations in your income.

- Again, add up how much you need for regular expenses each month, sticking to the essentials: food, transportation, rent, etc. Leave out the little luxuries you can live without in an emergency.

- Multiply that monthly amount by three: that's the amount you'll want to have on hand when an emergency strikes.

- Now start saving toward that amount. It's a good idea, if you can, to prioritize this account over other goals until you have raised the full three months' worth, even if it means being really frugal with your everyday spending for a while. You'll feel better knowing that an emergency in the future won't leave you unable to pay the rent!

- If your income fluctuates a lot, you may want to set yourself a 12-month goal for raising your emergency fund amount, and put aside more in the months when your income is high, less in months where your income dips.

- If you do have an emergency and dip into this fund, replace it as quickly as you can.

<u>BABY STEP 4</u>: Save for your goals. Here comes the payoff. If you have a spouse, you'll want to work together on this. Figure out what your major short-term and long-term goals are. Buying a car or jet-ski would be short-term. Paying off your mortgage or paying college tuition for your kids might be long-term. How much money will you need to achieve your dream?

How much can you start saving right now towards these goals?

Now that you've wrestled down your debt and put aside some rainy-day money, you may have some real cash to put aside for the future life you want.

HACK #6:

Commit to Tracking Money Relationship

"Help! I can't control my spending!"

If that's you, and all this talk about big future goals just leaves you feeling hopeless, there are some simple, classic methods to help you do a better job of sticking to the budget you've set for yourself.

Many people have a hard time sticking to commitments, whether they involve personal relationships or even resolutions they have made for themselves.

Your relationship with money has emotional dimensions, too. And sticking to your commitment to handle your money more responsibly may mean finding some practical ways to help you stay on track.

That is why writing it down on paper or on a digital spreadsheet as suggested earlier can help make your goals and progress more concrete.

<u>ASSIGNMENT</u>: Continue tracking your spending and recording it on the empty columns on your quickie budget, to see it you're living up to the spending goals you set for yourself. If you track your spending and saving patterns each month, you can see whether you're making progress on reining in your costs and maximizing your financial health. This can provide you with the incentive to stay on track.

HACK #7:
Mint Condition Budgeting

Another thing you can do is try budgeting software to help you keep track of your finances.

One highly recommended (and free!) system is Mint.com. You can sign up for an account on the website, and set it up to automatically record transactions occurring on your credit card and bank accounts (without allowing you to actually make transactions from the app). Using easy to understand graphics, it will help you keep track of your monthly spending, set budgets for various categories, calculate your net income (what you earned, minus your spending) each month, track your progress toward savings goals, and even track your net worth over time.

Watching your net worth rise month by month on a beautiful green bar chart may provide you with the incentive you need to stick to your plan.

You can use the website or download a handy app to use while you're on the go.

Ask questions before you sign up, however. Mint is popular and appears to be quite safe, but because signing up with Mint means handing over some (encrypted) information that allows read-only access to what's going on in your accounts, some smaller banks and other financial institutions don't allow access. Most major banks and investment brokers have special agreements with Mint to make this possible, so it's worth checking first. The Mint system can tell you whether the places you do business with are on their list.

ASSIGNMENT: Give Mint.com a try!

HACK #8:
The Cash Envelope Method

The envelope technique, which relies entirely on cash, is a simple way to help you set priorities and plan your finances effectively, especially if credit card debt has been a big part of your financial difficulties. It works for almost anyone, including people who don't handle a lot of money, like students or stay-at-home parents, and it's a great way to train yourself in money management.

Cut up your credit card, or at least take it out of your wallet and store it in a safe place at home for use in emergencies only.

Then follow these steps:

1. Use the quickie budget you set up for yourself (with 10% left over for savings).

2. Next, figure out how much you will need to save for your big but short-term GOALS (buy a car or a computer, take a vacation, etc.).

3. Decide how much you would like to set aside for undesignated long-term SAVINGS, to be used for bigger future goals, such as buying a home or retiring, and to be prepared for emergencies such as a sudden job loss or debilitating illness.

4. When you cash your paycheck, take the whole amount in cash.

5. Now prepare three envelopes, one for each category (EXPENSES, GOALS, SAVINGS).

6. In the first (envelope A, EXPENSES), put the amount of cash you will need for necessities for the next

month, based on the total you figured out in your quickie budget from HACK #3.

7. From the remaining cash, decide on an exact amount that you will put toward your short-term goals (placed in envelope B, GOALS) and the amount you will deposit into your long-term savings account (placed in envelope C, SAVINGS).

For the first while, your GOALS envelope will contain the amount you will be putting toward your baby steps (an emergency fund; then paying off debt; then putting aside three months' expenses).

Once you have made it through your baby steps, you can start saving toward short-term GOALS (buy a car or computer, take a vacation, etc.) and long-term SAVINGS (kids' college, house down payment, retirement, etc.)

- For example, if you earn $3,500 this month, $2,500 might go toward immediate living expenses. Out of

> the remainder, you might decide to invest $300 per month toward one or two of your short-term goals, and to put $200 per month into long-term savings.

If it helps when you're feeling deprived, you could decide to create a fourth envelope for mad money, a limited amount designated for items that make life fun, like that pair of shoes you've been wanting, concert tickets or lunch out with a friend. But be careful! When that envelope is empty, it's gone until the next month — do NOT dip into your other envelopes!

This envelope technique helps you manage your expenses, plan and save toward big purchases instead of going into debt, and set up a savings mechanism.

HACK #9:
The Percentage Pie Method

Instead of using specific amounts each month, you can use percentages to budget. It's an easy way to get a handle on where your money is going, especially if your income fluctuates from month to month.

Imagine your monthly income as a pie. Whatever the size of that pie, each of the three elements (expenses, goals, savings) will get a slice sized according to the percentage you've allotted to it.

Here's how it works:

1. Set percentages for each slice of the pie. For instance, the biggest proportion, half to three-quarters of it — 50% to 75% — typically goes to immediate expenses

(necessities like food, rent, insurance and so on). You might decide to put 10% into long-term savings, for expenses or projects that may be many years into the future. For shorter-term goals, say six months or two years away, you might put aside 25%. What's left of the pie is your discretionary spending, for non-necessities.

2. Now, each time you get paid you'll know what proportion of it should go into monthly expenses, goals, and savings.

3. Next, when your earnings are deposited into your bank account, transfer funds according to these percentages into separate accounts: a current one for living expenses, and savings accounts for your goals and long-term savings.

4. Repeat this process with every paycheck, and watch as your savings accounts grow into something you can feel good about! By sticking with this program, you'll

stop wasting money and feel a sense of fulfillment as you begin to see your financial goals take shape.

HACK #10:

Open Several Bank Accounts for Specialized Purposes

In the age of digital banking, it's easy and helpful to diversify your bank accounts to help you manage your money better. (Check with your bank on how you can do this without incurring extra costs.)

1. Do this once you've kept track of your spending to arrive at a total for monthly expenses, and created a plan for your short-term goals and long-term savings.

2. Open new accounts for designated purposes (no more than five), after checking with your bank to ensure this won't incur excessive fees. You might open a current account for bills; a savings account for short-

term goals; and a high-interest account for long-term savings. If you can, give each account an appropriate nickname on your bank website or app.

3. To keep it easy and avoid the temptation to spend money you want to save, set up automatic payments for bills (rent, utilities etc.), and automatic transfers to your savings accounts, going out on each payday. That way you'll never forget to take care of the essentials.

One more thing (just in case applicable to you): If you have a tendency to go crazy at the mall and get yourself into debt, do cut up your credit cards and ask your bank to set up withdrawal limitations with your savings accounts. To help them avoid the temptation to drain their bank accounts, chronic gamblers have the option to ask casinos to bar them entry. Do the same with your bank: go for options that will make it *impossible* to withdraw your hard-saved money too soon. Don't use your credit card unless you are sure you will be able to pay off the entire balance each and every month from the money you have allotted for discretionary spending.

This will make managing your money much easier, because technology can help you resist temptation.

HACK #11:
Use Credit Smartly, not Stupidly

Ever wonder why college kids with hardly any money in the bank get offers from credit card companies? Because there's big money to be made in consumer debt. The financial wizards know young people often go crazy when they get their first credit card, and it soon becomes an addiction.

There are more than a billion pieces of plastic riding at this moment in American wallets. Using those little cards makes it all too easy to spend more than you're earning, often on stuff you don't even need.

But getting deep into credit card debt is more than stressful: chances are, when you can't pay that bill next month you'll also be racking up a bad credit score, which can jeopardize your chances of being able to get credit when you really need it, say when you want to get a mortgage on that house you hope to buy.

- Credit cards are convenient and sometimes necessary, for example for buying products online, renting a car, or when an emergency hits and you don't have cash in your wallet. But credit card interest is extremely high and will quickly sink you if you can't afford to pay off your bill each and every month. So it's important to start out with a small limit so that you can't spend more than you can afford.

- Using a credit card responsibly will help you build up your credit score, which is how the banks measure your financial reliability. If on a particular month you find you can't pay off the whole bill, pay at least the minimum amount required ON TIME. And pay off the rest as soon as you can. Regular, on-time payments will keep you in good stead with the credit bureaus that track your reliability. Never, never, fail to make at least the minimum payment.

- Begin low. Beginning credit users might start with a $500 limit. The bank may offer higher limits to suck you in, but resist unless and until you are sure you can handle larger monthly payments.

- Avoid expensive cards. Beware the fine print on credit card offers, especially those that offer big perks like cash-back offers or airline points sufficient for a domestic flight. There's usually a big annual fee associated with a perk you may not really need. Keep your credit accounts to no more than two. And be careful about interest rates. If there's any chance you may not be able to pay the bill in full each month, that giant APR on the card is going to cost you dearly.

- Use a debit card instead. If you love the convenience of a credit card but hate being shocked by a big bill next month, you may find spending money you already have is your salvation. Use a card that's linked to the current account you've designated for living expenses for necessary items like groceries.

HACK #12:
Save Big Bucks by Avoiding Loans

If you have a car...

It's a familiar story. That car you've spent years paying off the loan for is finally all yours, and now it's starting to fall apart. You'd love to have a new car, but getting one now will put you back on the endless loan-repayment treadmill.

Car experts say that, as long as the car body itself isn't falling apart from rust, it's usually more economical to continue making repairs and doing maintenance as needed on an older vehicle than buying a new one. Besides, it's not at all uncommon these days for cars to rack up 200,000 or 300,000 miles without dying on the side of the road.

Sure, it might be nice to get into a shiny new vehicle with all the high-tech gadgetry. But it would also be nice to stay off that treadmill, wouldn't it?

Waiting a little longer for that new-car smell now could keep you off it forever!

- Consider whether you can keep the clunker going for another couple of years, and instead start putting the money you would have spent paying off another loan (or buying an even pricier lease) into a special savings account. When you finally do buy a car, watch the salesman's eyebrows go up as you tell him you won't need a loan, and chuckle at the big discount you'll get. Then drive home in that shiny new SUV and start putting your "loan" money into a savings account again for the next time — *earning* interest instead of paying it.

- And do consider buying a used vehicle. A new car loses a pile of its value the second it leaves the lot.

Why not let someone else take that hit, and buy a nice, low-mileage car that's a couple of years old? You'll save thousands on the purchase, some more on insurance, and still have a great vehicle that will get you where you need to go for years to come.

The overall principle here of saving instead of taking a loan (with the exception on your home or other investment assets) can apply to other big purchases that tend to depreciate over time.

A little delayed gratification can pay off for years and years to come.

HACK #13:
Know "Good Debt" from "Bad Debt"

If you're going to go into debt, try to stick to "good debt" — the kind that will set the stage for increased wealth in the future.

Real estate is often deemed "good debt" because, the recent recession to the contrary, it tends to appreciate in value, sometimes by a great deal. Plus, if you are investing in a home to live in, you are using that investment to underwrite your biggest monthly expense.

At today's low interest rates, you may do much better investing in real estate with a low-rate mortgage than by putting your money into financial products such as mutual funds. Paying off the mortgage on your family home is a worthy goal, but not a priority if you have other debts you need to deal with, or want to save toward other big purchases rather than add to your burden by taking out a loan.

Another kind of "good debt" is a student loan — provided you will use that loan to invest in an education that will increase your future earnings over what you might have earned without it. You are investing in YOU! To what degree a four-year college education pays off varies a great deal, of course, but on average college graduates earn a good deal more than people with only a high school diploma, over their lifetimes. Similarly, in an age when most people will need to change careers, or at least jobs, more than once, continuing education can pay off handsomely, even if you need to incur some debt to do it.

What's "bad debt"? Debt that involves depreciating assets.

Cars, for example, become less valuable the instant they leave the dealer's lot. Long before the loan is paid off, you've lost a heap of money. And don't even get started on boats. ("What are the two happiest days in a boat owner's life? The day he buys the boat. And the day he sells the boat.")

Worst debt? Payday loans, which are a legalized way to steal from the poor, with rates that often rise to something like 30% (though the lenders are at pains to hide the true cost of these short-term loans from you). Avoid them at all costs.

Next worst is credit card debt, which also comes at a high price. Make sure you can pay your billed balance off each and every month to avoid paying the high interest rate. If you find that impossible, cut up your cards or put them on a high shelf someplace, for use only in an emergency. Don't add a cent to your credit card balance until you've paid it off in full.

HACK #14:

Invest for the Future Now

Today's ultra-low interest rates can be discouraging if your main method for saving is a bank account or a CD.

Once you've gotten through the baby steps, consider investing in mutual funds or other vehicles that have the potential for much higher gains over the long run, and can help ensure a happier retirement.

A good way to start is by learning about your (U.S.) employer's 401k plan, if one is available to you.

- A 401k is a way to save and invest pre-tax income, meaning you don't have to pay tax on what you deposit into it until that far-off day when you retire and start taking the money (plus earnings) out. If that money comes out of your pay, you will see less tax taken off your paycheck and you'll hardly miss money you never saw to begin with.

Employers choose what investments are available within their 401k. Many also kick in some kind of matching funds for the amounts you put in voluntarily as an employee, making this is an ideal way to begin investing.

As your finances improve and you're able to think about investing in other vehicles, be sure to find yourself a good advisor who can help you determine your tolerance for risk and the best ways for you to invest, depending on how much you want to be involved in researching the options.

Many people invest in things like Exchange Traded Funds (ETF), which basically track common stock indices, have very low management fees, and require little attention on your part.

A Roth IRA, which is a basket of investments similar to a 401k except it uses post-tax income and allows your investment to grow tax-free, is another option to consider.

ASSIGNMENT: You are never too young to start securing your financial future, so explore some of these options for yourself to see which ones are right for you to put your money in.

HACK #15:

Proudly Put on Frugal Hat and Wear It with Pride

A lot of people talk about becoming more frugal when times are hard. But getting to that point isn't easy.

You'll need a lot of motivation, which starts with having a plan for a "financial fast."

- Think hard and be honest with yourself about what's getting in the way of your financial freedom — the unnecessary expenses that eat away at your financial stability, like dining out a lot, drinking fancy takeout coffee instead of making your own, or buying clothing at pricey stores.

ASSIGNMENT: If you're struggling financially, start by cutting at least some of those out of your list.

- Downscale your lifestyle. Living "big and comfy" is one thing, but consider whether all that instant gratification is preventing you from attaining your bigger goals, like getting out of debt, paying off your student loan, or moving into your dream home someday.

ASSIGNMENT: Try drawing a sort of motivational chart, listing your new restrictions (no more dining out every weekend, expensive shopping sprees, etc.) aligned with your new habits (buy clothing at thrift store, cook your own meals, etc.), followed by your final goal (buying a car, getting out of debt, etc.). Post this motivational chart somewhere prominent throughout your "financial fasting" period as a reminder to help you stick to the plan.

(BONUS) HACK #16:

Yield 20x Higher Interest with Online Banks

Still keeping your money in a brick-and-mortar bank? You might consider migrating to an online bank. Why? Because you'll earn up to 20 times higher interest than major players like Bank of America, Chase, Wells Fargo, and Citibank.

Here are a few online banks to get you started:

- Ally Bank (ally.com)
- CIT Bank ([cit.com](cit.com))
- Marcus by Goldman Sachs (marcus.com/us/en/savings)
- American Express (americanexpress.com/personalsavings)

- Discover (discover.com/online-banking)
- PurePoint (purepoint.com)

Because online banks lack marketing, promotion, and physical branches, most people simply haven't heard of them. On the flip side, this allows online banks to afford generous 2-3% interest rates that dwarf the average rates of even the biggest banks, which rarely ever go a trivial 0.05% for a savings account. (Keep in mind, though, that interest rates fluctuate in accordance with the Federal Reserve.) Plus, online banks typically have no maintenance fee and no minimum balance requirement.

Still on the fence about online banks? Rest assured that your money is safe, protected by the FDIC up to $250,000, as it would be in any other bank.

That said, and even with the attractive interest rates, online banking comes with its own set of inconveniences:

- No physical locations means you can't just walk into a branch whenever you need assistance or to speak with someone in person. Online banks do, however, offer 24-hour phone support.

- Without branded ATM machines, you're stuck using third-party ATMs and paying the appropriate fees every time you need to make a withdrawal. (Some online banks do offer reimbursements for those ATM fees.)

- Depositing money can also be a hassle without a physical branch. An extra workaround is usually needed to make deposits.

Our best advice is to use both traditional and online banks in tandem. Keep your traditional bank account active for convenience but open an online account for the monetary reward. Traditional banking makes a world of difference when transferring funds to and from your online accounts, since you can deposit and withdraw those funds at a physical branch.

ASSIGNMENT: Investigate some online banks, compare their current interest rates, and list the pros and cons of each with regard to your financial circumstances. Don't forget to research the other services they offer to make sure you have everything you need in one bank. For instance, if you don't have a credit card, you may want to consider only online banks with credit card offers, so you can manage your savings account and credit card under one virtual roof, without having to split your attention between two (or more) banks.

(ADVANCED BONUS) HACK #17:

Go from Newbie Investor to Building Wealth the Smart Investor's Way

Are you one of the lucky ones with extra cash peeking out from under their pillow? If so, then investing in funds and stocks might just be for you.

If you've never invested before, you may be overwhelmed with apprehension. Given all the negative press about the risks involved, it's all we can do to brace ourselves for yet another recession just around the proverbial corner. (Then again, when has the media ever put a positive spin on the financial market?)

For what it's worth, any kind of investment carries with it a bit of uncertainty, but no more so than the possibility of having your money become worthless through inflation or being a victim of theft.

It might seem counterintuitive, but any "bad news" you hear during market downturns or recessions is actually a prime signal to take advantage of major discounts when everybody else is leaving the market. History tells us that just as the market is sure to drop, so will it bounce back. The most fundamental investing strategy is as relevant as ever: buy low and sell high. In other words, take dips in the market as opportunities to snatch up stocks and, once the market recovers, liquidate them for a profit.

What's the best way to enter the stock market?

With so many components to consider, each as individual as the investor aiming to use them, this isn't some definitive guide on investing (and those who claim to have one just want your money, which is better injected into the market anyway). Still, there are some crucial things to keep in mind when getting started.

Newbies do well to invest in funds and government bonds over company stocks. As safer and easier options, they require little in the way of technical analysis. Our strategic suggestion is to go for an S&P 500 index fund and throw in a few government bonds for the long term. (For those unfamiliar, S&P stands for Standard & Poor's, a financial agency that originated in 1860 and later developed its market index, known today as the S&P 500, as the premier indicator of market performance.)

In the words of the master himself, Warren Buffet: "Put 10% of the cash in short-term government bonds and 90% in a very low-cost S&P 500 index fund."

So long as you keep the long term in mind, ignoring all the distractions of what may or may not be the next big things by investing in an index fund, you'll have security on your side. Companies come and go, but the S&P 500 will always be there to substitute defunct or cash-poor companies with the next contenders worthy of their coveted spots in the top 500.

The S&P 500 is ideal for long-term investing because it survived the Great Depression of the 1930s and the Financial Crisis of 2008, producing solid returns for those who followed it and held on to their investments, as attested by the S&P 500's historical performance to the present day (macrotrends.net/2324/sp-500-historical-chart-data).

Where can you invest?

In the past, one would need to have walked into a brokerage firm, hired a broker, and paid all the necessary fees that essentially paid the broker's salary. For a long time, this barrier to entry dissuaded many from even bothering to try. Not so today. Thanks to modern technologies and such online tools as Robinhood (robinhood.com) and M1 Finance (m1finance.com), commissions are a thing of the past. Just sign up, put your money in, and allow it to grow passively (no day trading here).

Looking for something more involved? Start investing your savings in a retirement account like the Roth IRA as your primary account, followed by a normal brokerage account. An IRA account, unlike its brokerage counterpart, gives you special tax benefits. If you ever win the lottery, most financial advisors will tell you that maxing out your IRA every year should be your first priority. (As of 2019, yearly contributions are capped at $6,000.) A Roth IRA may just be the best investment of your life, because it's the easiest way for average folks to steadily build long-term wealth. The amount you earn compounds exponentially over time through appreciation and dividend payouts (as loyalty incentives from companies for retaining their stock shares) if you reinvest those dividends back into your account to buy more shares, resulting in a "layering" of compounded interests.

The most important thing is to get started now, because time really is money. As with the S&P 500, had you started earlier, the higher your returns would have been today.

ASSIGNMENT: Visit your nearest or preferred brokerage firm and start investing today! If you want to do everything yourself or don't like paying brokerage fees, we recommend signing up with Robinhood or M1 Finance.

(ADVANCED BONUS) HACK #18:

Diversify Money into Alternative Savings Accounts

Another way to save your money without banks is through Betterment (betterment.com) and Wealthfront (wealthfront.com). While both are additional investing platforms that you would use like Robinhood or M1 Finance, they share the advantage of managing your cash like a savings account that earns you interest upwards of 2% (higher than some online banks) and is also covered by FDIC insurance.

While these are *not* banks, they nevertheless offer FDIC insurance by channeling your money through the bona fide banks they've partnered with. Think of them as a bridge connecting to banks where your money is actually being stored. They're able to offer such high interest rates to begin with because their partnered banks take your money and use it, as banks do, to make money on their own through loans with interest rates as high as 10%. They get a portion of that through the act of referral before passing on the rest to you.

Although Betterment and Wealthfront offer investment opportunities, you may choose to use them solely as savings platforms. But why, you might be wondering, not take advantage of their investment opportunities? Because they do charge a small percentage fee, whereas investing with Robinhood and M1 Finance is completely free. The only reason Betterment and Wealthfront even offer such generous interest rates for saving with them is to encourage you to invest through them, thus allowing them to gouge you with fees.

Does this mean you should take all of your money from your regular or online banks and put it into these FDIC-insured savings accounts? Absolutely not! They're not intended to be used as substitutes for your bank but are more like escrows in savings account clothing, with money readily available for investing. Moreover, these savings accounts are still in their infancy, so the rules could change at any given time.

Assuming you're not using Betterment and Wealthfront for their investing features (unless you're fine with the investment percentage fee), they simply give you more ways to diversify how you save your money.

ASSIGNMENT: Check out Betterment and Wealthfront and decide whether either is a great fit for you. They can change their services and rates at any time, so it's important to stay updated.

INFO UNLOCKED:
Wiser Money Management

Managing money is a crucial life skill. To be able to earn money is one thing, but finding ways to handle it wisely and somehow multiply it is another.

Applying all of these aforementioned strategies will help ensure that you have some saved for "rainy days," your golden years, and of course to leave to loved ones when you don't need it anymore.

You work so hard to earn your money; wouldn't it be great if you could take full advantage of it?

So, from now on, plan your financial future, budget your expenses, motivate yourself to stick to a budget, and maybe even live a little more frugally until you're really on track.

Go ahead and be your own financial manager and take control of your financial life.

Money Management and Budgeting Hacks

www.ingramcontent.com/pod-product-compliance
Lightning Source LLC
Chambersburg PA
CBHW061200180526
45170CB00002B/889